In the name of Allah
Most Gracious Most Merciful

Better Than A Thousand Months:
An American Muslim Family Celebration

By Hassaun Ali Jones-Bey

IBN MUSA PUBLISHING

Blessings
&
Best wishes
Hassaun A. Jones-Bey

Ibn Musa Publishing

Library of Congress Catalog Card Number:
96-94713

ISBN: 0-9654248-0-4

IBN MUSA, INC.
P.O. BOX 424
FREMONT, CA 94537-0424
Phone: (510) 745-8221
Fax: (510) 739-6873
E-mail: IBNMUSA@AOL.COM

DEDICATION

This book is dedicated to Noble Drew Ali (d. 1924), who gave his life in the struggle for human dignity and freedom of worship. This book is also dedicated to many other determined African Americans, living and dead, who have struggled courageously toward the same goals. By the Grace of Allah, their sacrifices have paved the way for me to write and publish this lighthearted book about an African-American family celebrating the Islamic fast and feast of Ramadan. Imam Waritheen Muhammad has described such people as "pioneers" of Al-Islam in America. May Allah forgive their sins and reward them with success in this life and the next.

ACKNOWLEDGMENTS

Writing and publishing this book has been a family project. So to everyone in my family I am deeply grateful for the inspiration, material as well as moral support, editing and other forms of critique, along with the tireless assistance that you have provided with the innumerable details that go into a published book.

Special thanks also go to my good friends Hilal Sala, Rasheed Patch, Kathleen Lawrence, Hafsah Al-Amin and Imam Abu Qadir Al-Amin, as well as to Ali Ramadan Abuzakuk of Amana Publications who took the time to read the manuscript carefully and to provide invaluable assistance, advice and encouragement.

To many others who have helped me but are not mentioned here, I also extend my thanks. Of course all thanks are actually due to Allah, the Source of all the good that you may find in this book as well as the Source of forgiveness for any mistakes or shortcomings.

Contents

The names **Allah** and **Muhammad** (**may Allah bless him and grant him peace**).

INTRODUCTION

This book is about an American Muslim family, the Harris-Beys, who are celebrating the holy month of Ramadan. Ramadan is one of two major Muslim holidays. The other one occurs during the annual pilgrimage to Mecca.

This is not an instruction book, a religious text, a documentary or even a family memoir. It's just a story. It's based on real events and real personalities, but the characters' names have been changed, and events have been added or exaggerated to turn it into an enjoyable story. It would be great if I could say that this is a love story or an adventure story, but if I did, it wouldn't be true. This is actually what I call a family story.

When my children were very young, I used to tell them stories. We would sit in a circle on the living room floor, and I would strum and finger-pick a series of easy chords on my guitar. While playing, I would tell a story, making it up as I went along. My children and any others who happened to be with them would become the characters in the story. I thought my stories were corny, but the kids loved them and would always clamor for another as soon as I was finished. It was exhausting.One time the kids got so excited that one of them jumped onto my guitar and broke it. To my surprise, the guitar still played. It just never looked quite the same.

My kids even started to tell stories of their own. They would dress up in swathes of colored material their grandmother had sent them and would put on plays. One of them would be the narrator, and they would make up the plays as they went along. They would invite the adults to come and watch the plays, which were often quite good. If you don't mind a corny joke every now and then, family storytelling can be very entertaining. I recommend it.

This family story started out as a short performance for my daughter's third grade class. As I told the story, I recited from the Muslim scripture, the Qur'an, to give my audience a feel for the beauty of the celebration. The youngsters enjoyed it, and I had a great time. I had so much fun that I kept writing after the performance was done and turned my story into a book.

In this book, pages of Qur'anic calligraphy take the place of recitation in the storytelling, and landscape photography shows the changing light during the night that the story takes place. I've also resisted the temptation to fill the book full of cute-kid pictures, to keep browsers from mistaking it for a photo album or Big Daddy's Brag Book. The idea here is just to share some enjoyable family and religious experiences with anyone who has the time and inclination for a pleasant read.

So much for the introduction. Now it's storytelling time. Take your shoes off and have a seat in my living room. Enjoy yourself. But please, try not to get too excited.

A FATHER'S DREAM

"Whoa, heck of a time for an earthquake." My forehead bounces off the train window as I look out and guess that it's about 40 feet down to the West Oakland Post Office. For once I wish I were waiting on line in the post office instead of waiting for take-off in an elevated train packed with commuters. My forehead bounces off the window again, but I don't move right away. I figure this bump won't matter much if the shaking doesn't stop soon. I begin to pray, "In the name of Allah, Most Gracious, Most Merciful." The shaking stops. I keep praying, "All praise is due to Allah the Lord of all the worlds..."

I slowly become aware of people around me. It seems as if we all are becoming aware of each other. As if on cue, we all start checking to see if everybody is all right. One woman is trying to gather wrapping paper and gifts that have spilled out of her shopping bag. It's the first week in November, and the department stores in downtown San Francisco have already put up their Christmas decorations. *The electrical power in the train is not back on yet, so we can't go anywhere, and the conductor can't tell us any more about the smoking brakes that had marooned us here before the earthquake made us feel like the inside of a milkshake. I'm not too concerned, though. Not because I'm brave. Just because I'm too far behind on my sleep. Long hours at work. Lots to do at home. I notice a glowing red ball of sun sinking into the western mountains. "What a deal," I think. "Can I go to bed now, too?"*

I close my eyes and chuckle. I imagine my guardian angel as a great hypnotist with the sun ball on the end of his watch chain. He is making it swing slowly like a pendulum. I hear his smiling voice, "You are getting sleepy...."

"Why don't Muslims celebrate Christmas, Dad?" my daughter asked.

As Nora Maryam spoke, we stopped at a red light. I looked across the front seat of our pickup truck only to see the back of her head. She was gazing wistfully out of the window at the brightly colored Christmas lights and decorations. I smiled. I was also hearing her other question, the one she hadn't asked.

It was a little after sunset, and we were driving past a shopping center near San Francisco. The stores were full of people buying gifts. Even the jazz station on our truck radio was playing Christmas carols. The flatbed of our pickup was full of wood for our fireplace at home. The sunset, the lights, the music. It all felt so ... so ... magic.

When I didn't answer right away, Maryam turned to look at me. She saw my smile and returned it. She knew I was going to tell her a story. And I happen to be a pretty good storyteller. Right about then the light turned green and we continued on our way.

"You've got a point, Sweetie," I said, still smiling. "We Muslims believe that Jesus (Peace be upon him) was a Word from God, just like the Christians do. And the night when God's Word was born was such a good night that we definitely have to celebrate it. No question about it."

"Huh?" she asked, mouth hanging open. I congratulated myself for catching her off guard. It's not easy. We parked the car on our favorite street with a view of the San Francisco Bay and got out for a stroll.

"Do you know how good that night was?" I asked, taking her hand.

"No. Tell me," she said pertly, having fully recovered from her brief moment of surprise.

"It was better than a thousand months," I said. Then I began to recite to her from Muslim scripture, the Qur'an, which Muslims learn to recite from memory in classical Arabic. After each Arabic verse, I explained the English meaning.

In the name of God who gives before we ask,
yet if we ask forgives and still gives more.
Surely, We sent it down in a night of perfect
measure.
And do you know what the night of perfect
measure is?
The night of perfect measure is better than a
thousand months.
The angels and the Holy Spirit descend in
that night.
With the permission of their Lord on every
errand
With peace, until the rise of dawn. (97:1-5)

She looked at me. "That sounds almost like a
Christmas carol," she said. "Is it really from the
Qur'an?"

"Yup," I answered, warming up to the evening
magic. "Once upon a time in Arabia, there was a
young man who had such a pure heart, and who was
so kind, honest and brave that everyone, even his
enemies, called him Al-Amin, which means the
trustworthy one."

"That's the Prophet Muhammad," she said.

بِسْمِ ٱللَّهِ ٱلرَّحْمَٰنِ ٱلرَّحِيمِ

إِنَّا أَنزَلْنَاهُ فِى لَيْلَةِ ٱلْقَدْرِ ۝

وَمَا أَدْرَاكَ مَا لَيْلَةُ ٱلْقَدْرِ ۝

لَيْلَةُ ٱلْقَدْرِ خَيْرٌ مِّنْ أَلْفِ شَهْرٍ ۝

تَنَزَّلُ ٱلْمَلَائِكَةُ وَٱلرُّوحُ فِيهَا

بِإِذْنِ رَبِّهِم مِّن كُلِّ أَمْرٍ ۝

سَلَامٌ هِىَ حَتَّىٰ مَطْلَعِ ٱلْفَجْرِ ۝

"Not quite," I replied. "He didn't actually become the Prophet until the night of perfect measure. He was 40 years old then, and that's when God sent the beginning of the Qur'an into his heart.

"That was during the month of Ramadan," I continued. "That's when these beautiful words from God that we learn and chant and live by were born into the heart of our Prophet. For the sake of that single night, we give up eating and drinking during the daytime for the entire month of Ramadan. And we think that is a big thing. But in reality that night is greater than a thousand months. That's more than 80 years. It's greater than a lifetime."

She stopped walking and looked at me.

"Did all of the words in the Qur'an come from God?" she asked.

"Yup," I answered. "They came down in the pure heart of the Prophet Muhammad, just like Jesus came down to the pure virgin Mary (May Allah grant them all blessings and peace)."

We started walking again and my attention drifted out over the bay.

Red and white ribbons of head and tail lights chased across the Oakland Bay Bridge and Golden Gate Bridge, while strings of Christmas lights draped the skyscrapers in downtown San Francisco and Emeryville. Navigation lights on airliners approaching the San Francisco airport from the east made me think of wise men approaching a manger. Maryam grasped my hand with both of hers and tugged my thoughts back to her next question.

"Then why do we fast during Ramadan, while Christians sing songs and buy things at Christmas?"

"Because the Qur'an says so, Sweetie."

"Yes, Daddy," she blurted. "The Qur'an tells us to fast during Ramadan. What I want to know is *why* the Qur'an tells us to fast. Does it explain that?"

"Patience," I said. How does an 8-year-old formulate such complex questions? I think she'll grow up to be a lawyer. Or better yet, a judge of Islamic law. It's a lot harder to tell a story to someone when it's interactive. Maybe I ought to buy her a computer.

"I am trying to be patient," she sighed.

"I know, Sweetie, and that's good," I said. "That's why we fast: to learn patience."

Then I recited from the Qur'an again:

Oh you who believe
fasting has been prescribed for you
As it was prescribed for those before you
So that you will be conscious of God. (2:183)

"How does fasting make you conscious of God?" she asked. "Why couldn't we raise our consciousness by giving and getting nice presents?"

"Patience is the answer to both of your questions," I smiled. Why should she settle for being a lawyer or an Islamic judge, when she could be president of the United States?

"But why is patience so important, Daddy?"

I looked at her without answering. That was a hard one. My glance drifted back to the vibrant and colorful San Francisco Bay at night. It was as though I could count every one of the thousand spectacular months in this one beautiful night. But exactly where was my peaceful night? I knew that I was standing in

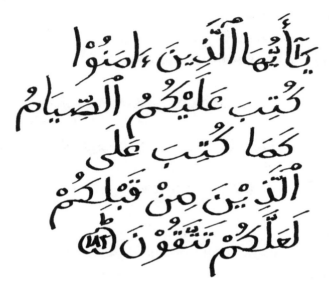

بِسْمِ ٱللَّهِ ٱلرَّحْمَٰنِ ٱلرَّحِيمِ

يَٰٓأَيُّهَا ٱلَّذِينَ ءَامَنُوا۟ كُتِبَ عَلَيْكُمُ ٱلصِّيَامُ كَمَا كُتِبَ عَلَى ٱلَّذِينَ مِن قَبْلِكُمْ لَعَلَّكُمْ تَتَّقُونَ ۝

it, but I certainly couldn't find it in this jumble of chattering months.

"Is this one of those things that I'll understand when I get older?" she asked in such a mature way that I picked her up and hugged her. She is actually getting a little heavy for me to pick up. But I still like to play the big strong daddy every now and then.

I put her down and dropped to one knee so that I could look directly in her eyes. I smiled like a mischievous old elf (Christmas spirit, and all that kind of thing, you know) and said in a deep and jolly voice, "Maryam, you already know why patience is important."

Of course she looked back at me as if wondering, "What's this nut up to now?" She must have gotten that look from her mother.

"You must have forgotten," I continued, warming up to my part. "Come for a ride in my time machine," I said, standing up and walking towards our truck. "Perhaps we can jog your memory."

"Time machine! What time machine?!" she shouted, running after me and grabbing my hand. I chuckled. The future president of the United States was still my beloved 8-year-old daughter -- for a little while, anyway.

صَلَّى ٱللهُ عَلَيْهِ وَ سَلَّمَ

TIME TRAVEL I

"Why did you turn the radio off?" Maryam asked as I started up the truck.

"It interferes with the operation of the time machine," I said. "It's just like on an airplane, when they ask you to turn off devices that might interfere with the navigation equipment."

"There's no navigation equipment on this old pickup truck," she laughed.

"This isn't a pickup truck right now," I said. "It just looks like one. Whenever I touch the radio switch just right, the pickup turns into a time machine."

"Did you have to pay extra for that feature?" she asked coolly.

"No, Mrs. President, they tried to charge me for it. But I drove a tough bargain." My time machine was obviously pointing in the wrong direction. After a quick check for oncoming traffic, I made an abrupt U-turn out of my parking space.

"Daddy, you just crossed a double yellow line," she said. "Isn't that illegal?"

"Not in a time machine," I answered. "Time machines move fast, even when you think you are standing still. If you point one in the wrong direction for too long, though, the results could be disastrous."

I popped a tape in the cassette player, and listened to a very dear friend from Senegal in West Africa recite the Qur'an. His voice has a way of making people sit quietly and get all starry-eyed. The stars in the sky started to shine brighter too, as we headed away from the city lights and into the nearby mountains.

One thing I love about the San Francisco Bay Area, even more than the weather, is the landscape. No matter which way you turn, you can see mountains rising peacefully in the distance. And if you drive for just a few minutes, you can often find one of those peaceful spots for yourself. Tonight, I raced off to fill my sky with stars before Maryam became too sleepy to hear the rest of my tale.

"Do you know what a parable is, Sweetie?"

"Isn't is some kind of story?"

Great, she's still awake.

"That's right, honey. It's a story with a message in it. That's what we're doing tonight, telling a story with a message. And we're coming to the best part of the story. Do you know why it's the best part?"

"No."

"Because you're going to tell it."

"Me?"

"Yes, you. So pay attention and keep watching the sky; there's a parable there about patience. And in a few minutes, when I stop the truck, you're going to have to tell me what it means."

"Okay, Daddy."

Finally I had the time machine pointed in the right direction. As we arrived at our destination, I drove the truck into the parking lot in a campground that we visit sometimes. I turned the truck off and we got out to let our eyes adapt to the dark. As they did, the sky filled with stars, and stars, and nothing else. I lifted Nora Maryam up so that she could sit on one of the logs in the back of the truck. I leaned against the truck and looked up with her.

"This really is a time machine," she said. "It's so beautiful and quiet out here. It's chilly too."

I pulled a blanket from behind the seats in the cab, and threw it over her shoulders.

"Is this like the night that Jesus was born, and like the night that the Qur'an was revealed?"

I smiled. She gets her story-telling talent from her old man.

"It's so peaceful and quiet," I agreed. "As if it's waiting patiently..."

"For God's Word to be born," she sparkled like a triumphant little scientist.

"That's right," I continued. "The Virgin Mary and the Prophet Muhammad (Peace be upon them) both left the rush and noise of the city behind. They let everybody else rush around, while they waited quietly

and peacefully, on a night just like this beautiful night. And then God's Word came to them.

"Do you see that star light Nora Maryam? That's what your name means. We named you after the light that came to Mary."

It's always hard to tell if kids hear you, when you're pouring your heart out and telling them what you think are the most important words in the world. She was looking up and pondering who knows what. Then she yawned, and I didn't have to wonder about her thoughts anymore. It was bed time for Maryam, and she was fading fast. I helped her down from the flatbed and back into the cab of the pickup.

She settled into the passenger seat, smiled sleepily and asked, "Do you think that if we learn to be patient like this night, that God's Word will come to us too?"

"We are God's Words," I answered. "In the Qur'an God says that whenever He wants to create anything or anyone, he simply says 'Be.' And here we are."

I closed her door and decided to take the time machine home by the scenic route. I walked around to the driver's side, and before climbing in, I pulled a prayer rug out from behind the seat and spread it on the ground. I took off my shoes, stood on the prayer rug, and made my evening prayer beneath the great dome of Allah's universal mosque. When I climbed in to drive home, I didn't turn on the tape player. I recited from the Qur'an to myself:

When the angels said:

O Mary, surely Allah gives thee good news with a word from Him

Whose name is the Messiah, Jesus, son of Mary,

Worthy of regard in this world and the Hereafter,

And of those who are drawn nigh to Allah.

And he will speak to the people when in the cradle

and when of old age, and he will be one of the good ones.

She said: My Lord, how can I have a son and man has not yet touched me?

He said: Even so: Allah creates what He pleases.

When He decrees a matter, He only says to it BE. and it is.(3:45-47)

بِسْمِ اللّٰهِ الرَّحْمٰنِ الرَّحِيْمِ

إِذْ قَالَتِ الْمَلٰٓئِكَةُ يٰمَرْيَمُ

إِنَّ اللّٰهَ يُبَشِّرُكِ بِكَلِمَةٍ مِّنْهُ

اسْمُهُ الْمَسِيْحُ عِيْسَى ابْنُ مَرْيَمَ

وَجِيْهًا فِى الدُّنْيَا وَالْاٰخِرَةِ

وَمِنَ الْمُقَرَّبِيْنَ ۙ

وَيُكَلِّمُ النَّاسَ فِى الْمَهْدِ

وَكَهْلًا وَّمِنَ الصّٰلِحِيْنَ ۩

قَالَتْ رَبِّ اَنّٰى يَكُوْنُ لِيْ وَلَدٌ

وَّلَمْ يَمْسَسْنِيْ بَشَرٌ ۗ

قَالَ كَذٰلِكِ اللّٰهُ يَخْلُقُ مَا يَشَاءُ ۚ

إِذَا قَضٰٓى أَمْرًا فَإِنَّمَا يَقُوْلُ

لَهُ كُنْ فَيَكُوْنُ ۩

33

By this time, we were passing the shopping center again and were within a few miles of home. I switched on the jazz radio station to find Nat King Cole crooning some seasonal favorites. Maryam stirred sleepily and seemed to be asking me something, almost as in a dream.

I stopped at the red light and looked over at her. She was looking at me and smiling, so I turned down the radio and asked, "What did you say?"

"How many shopping days until Ramadan?"

I jumped at the blast of a horn behind me, and noticed that the light had turned green.

صلَّى اللهُ عَلَيْهِ وَ سَلَّم

37

OATMEAL DELIGHT

I open my eyes and see a green traffic light through the train window. The sun has gone down. The lights have come on in the train and people are cheering. They stop cheering as the train lurches into motion for the first time since the big milkshake. But they begin cheering again when the train continues to move along the tracks in a smooth, straight line. If I wore a watch I would know how late I am for this evening's Boy Scout meeting. On second thought, there's probably not going to be a meeting tonight.

The conductor informs us over the intercom to check for our belongings before leaving the train at the next station. Evidently through-service has not been restored yet. So everyone will have to get off at the next station and continue our commutes on buses. This is going to be a long night. I wonder how long I was asleep, as my still-sluggish limbs shuffle stiffly out of the train and toward the waiting buses.

I settle into a seat on the bus as my thoughts continue to churn. "San Francisco scenery is nice," I chuckle to myself. "But it's expensive." As the bus begins to move, I look forward to another nap on the way home. I think about leisurely weekends, the kind I used to have before starting my second job. My thoughts begin to fade into just one. I smile as my great hypnotist lifts the bus into the air and rocks it back and forth like a cradle. I hear him singing, "Rockabye Ahmed...."

"Hey Dad, Maryam said you took her for a ride in your time machine last night. Has she been eating vegetarian pizzas with peanut butter balls and rocky road ice cream again?"

News travels fast. On weekend days, as everybody migrates back to bed after dawn prayers, I normally head to the kitchen to prepare one of my critically acclaimed breakfasts. Every now and then, however, somebody volunteers to be assistant cook, and this assistant had a lot of questions. Even the best of storytellers needs some quiet time occasionally. So I ignored my younger son's questions and told him to chop more apples for our pot of oatmeal delight.

Muhammad was not to be deterred, however. "She said you've got a switch on the radio in the pickup truck. What's the deal, Dad?"

"Patience," I said. Since I didn't feel like talking, I tried a one-word answer. But the one that seemed to work last night didn't work today.

"Yeah," Muhammad replied. "That's what Maryam said. Something about sitting patiently under the stars."

"Right," I said. "I understand what she's trying to say, and it would be good to sort out some of the details. But it would be best if I only had to say this once. So why don't we wait until after breakfast and get together in the living room for another time machine ride."

"Great, Dad." Muhammad is always ready for adventures. Probably because he plays so much Nintendo.

"But how are we going to get the pickup truck into the living room?" he asked. He's always so practical, too. Maybe that's why he manages to win at Nintendo.

"We don't have to, buddy," I said. "We can use the radio on the bookcase."

"Neat. I'll tell the others." He took off out of the kitchen so fast that I thought I could actually see little dust circles behind him. One of us had been reading too many comic books.

Oh well, back to storytelling. At least I didn't have to make any of this stuff up. It's already written in books on religion and history. My job was just to weave the strands together, so that my young and restless audience could understand and enjoy it.

It's bad enough when people tell you to eat stuff that you don't like because it's good for you. But life can really get bad when you have to listen to things you don't like to hear, too. And it's seldom necessary. My personal view is that half of the evil in the world is caused by bad cooks and the other half is caused by bad storytellers.

Take my oatmeal delight for instance. I think all kids go through a stage where they make pained faces at any food that is not either hamburgers or candy. When my 16-year-old son, Ibrahim, was 2 years old, he used to hate beans but love burritos. All of the kids grew up hating both fresh fruit and oatmeal. But if you chop the fruit up and cook it into the oatmeal, they can't get enough of it. Especially if you tell them that it ain't oatmeal, but oatmeal delight.

مُحَمَّد

صَلَّى ٱللَّهُ عَلَيْهِ وَ سَلَّمَ

SMILING BELLIES

As it happens, there is no better audience to sit around with on a sunny living room floor and tell stories to than a pack of fat little bellies full of warm oatmeal ... excuse me, oatmeal delight ... banana bread and sassafras tea.

"Now you guys all know the story of the Prophet Muhammad (May Allah bless him and grant him peace) in the cave, when the angel Gabriel came to him with the first verses of the Qur'an, right?

"Well Ramadan starts in about a month, and the question has come up as to why we remember that event by fasting. So I thought it might be a good idea to explain it. First though, let's explain what we are *not* doing when we fast. Can anybody tell me that?"

Hmmm. Nothing but smiling bellies. Not even wisecrack answers. They must have eaten more oatmeal than I thought. I hope they don't fall back asleep. Wait, Muhammad is starting to perk up. Now we'll get some life into this discussion.

"Dad, When can we turn on the time machine?"

"I'm glad you brought that up, Muhammad." count on Mr. Detail to make my life difficult. The bellies are beginning to pay attention, though.

"Actually, the question I just asked you is a bit of a riddle. Before I can let all of you guys into the time machine, I have to make sure that you're all awake enough to handle the ride. So let's make a go of it. If you were watching someone fast, and didn't know why they were doing it, what might you think they were doing?"

"I'd call it starving," said Aaliah Raheemah, my cerebral and artistic 14-year old daughter.

"Thank you, Aaliah," I said. "That's quite right. And why would you call it starving?"

"Because it's just going without food," said Aliyah Rahmah, Aaliah's athletic and enterprising stepsister who happens to be the same age. "And that's what starving is."

Such impeccable logic. These two are going to be university professors.

"Okay crew," I said. "You've done quite well with this riddle.

"Allah wants us to fast, but He does not want us to practice starvation. For instance, people who would have a hardship fasting because they are ill or on a journey are allowed to eat during the day in Ramadan and make their fast up on other days. And people who cannot fast at all, possibly because they are elderly, or because of physical conditions like diabetes that require them to eat regularly, can feed a poor person for each day of Ramadan instead of fasting. Allah also says that He has no need of fasting from people who insist on being foul-mouthed and ornery while they do it."

Then I recited from the Qur'an:

Allah wants things to be easy for you and does not want any hardship for you
And He desires that you complete the number of days for the fast
and that you should exalt the Greatness of Allah for having guided you
and that you may give thanks. (2:185)

"Now can we start up the time machine, Dad?" asked Muhammad, by way of reminding me of the specific event that he would like to be thankful for. "And can I drive?"

"No, I want to drive," said Maryam.

"If these guys are driving, I'll hide under the back seat, thank you," said Ibrahim, my computer genius son with the Mister Spock smile.

"We're all going to drive," I said. "The living room time machine works like a starship. It takes a whole crew to drive it." I flash my own little Mr. Spock smile, while watching signs of growing interest percolate across the faces of my Star Trek fanatics.

50

بِسْمِ اللَّهِ الرَّحْمَٰنِ الرَّحِيمِ

يُرِيدُ اللَّهُ بِكُمُ الْيُسْرَ وَلَا يُرِيدُ بِكُمُ الْعُسْرَ وَلِتُكْمِلُوا الْعِدَّةَ وَلِتُكَبِّرُوا اللَّهَ عَلَىٰ مَا هَدَاكُمْ وَلَعَلَّكُمْ تَشْكُرُونَ ۝

"As we approach our destination, I will tell you about the situation and the personalities of the people involved. Then each one of you will have to be one of the personalities. And you'll have to deal with the situation in the same way as a person with those values would deal with it.

"So it's like role playing," Aaliah observed with her characteristic air of sophisticated detachment.

"We did role playing in Mrs. Mugwart's class last week..." began Aliyah.

"That's great dear," I interrupted what was likely to become a very entertaining, but very long story. "So you should find this right up your alley.

"Now we are going to visit the Prophet Muhammad in a cave outside of Mecca, when the angel Gabriel brought him the very beginning of the Qur'an. Does everybody understand the plan? Good.

"Okay Maryam, you come with me over to the radio, so we can adjust the knob and get started."

TIME TRAVEL II

"Okay crew, we are traveling to a cave outside of Mecca, during the month of Ramadan about 1400 years ago. When we arrive, the landing party will beam down and take up their roles. The angel Gabriel, played by Aaliah, will visit the Prophet Muhammad, played by Maryam, and will tell him to recite.

"The narrator for this portion of our story, played by our own little Muhammad, will read from this book about the Prophet Muhammad. He will tell our characters what to do, and keep the whole thing from getting too far out of hand.

"The other characters in our story include the prophet's wife Khadijah, played by Aliyah, and Khadijah's cousin, the old holy man named Waraqah, played by Ibrahim.

"Now here are their qualities: The Prophet (May Allah bless him and grant him peace) is very honest and very patient. Lady Khadijah (May Allah be pleased with her) is very wise and very loving. The angel Gabriel exists only to do God's will. Waraqah (May Allah be pleased with him) is very wise and very religious.

"Okay, Muhammad ... excuse me, I mean Mr. Narrator ... Take it away."

"Excuse me, Dad," Muhammad said. "I think we have a problem here."

"Oh really? What's the problem, Muhammad?"

"We can't do a role play."

"No problem, buddy." I was impatient to start and did not want to be bothered with details. "This isn't a real role play. It's a time machine ride."

"Really, Dad," Muhammad persisted. "We read this story last week at our Islamic Sunday School, and we asked the teacher if we could do a role play. He said that Muslims should not make any pictures of the Prophet Muhammad or of angels and that includes taking their roles in a play."

"Then how are people supposed to get a real feel for what happened?" I did not disguise my frustration.

"With their minds," Muhammad answered.

"I think that there's an oil leak in the time machine," I said.

"I think we need a referee," Aliyah responded. "We can all say the different parts and imagine what actually happened. Muhammad can be the narrator to make sure we don't say anything wrong. Mom can be the referee to make sure that nobody tries to act out their part."

Everybody seemed to think this was a great idea and charged off to get my wife. Nobody had asked my opinion, but it was starting to sound like a soccer game to me. It took an effort for me to stay quiet when my wife arrived in a black and white striped dress and a baseball cap. Maryam handed her the pitch pipe that I use to tune my guitar.

"Here's your whistle," she said.

Muhammad handed her a dishtowel.

"And here's your flag," he smiled.

Without a word from me, everyone took their places. Muhammad nodded at me and smiled. Then he began to read in a loud and clear voice, "Even before he received his first revelation, the Prophet Muhammad would occasionally spend several days at a time meditating in the nearby mountains."

Since we would all be using our imaginations, I closed my eyes and listened.

Muhammad continued reading. "It was during one of these periods in the month of Ramadan, when the prophet was 40 years old, that the angel Gabriel approached Muhammad and said ....."

I heard Aaliah the artist's voice say, "Recite!" But for some reason, I was imaging a powerful cat eyeing a delicious mouse.

Maryam's voice replied, "I do not recite."

My imaginary cat smiled.

The narrator continued reading. "The angel then wrapped his arms around Muhammad's chest and squeezed the Prophet until he could barely breathe."

My imaginary cat pounced.

A blast from the pitch pipe brought me back into

the room. I opened my eyes to see Aaliah engulfing Maryam in a no-nonsense bear hug. I guess she couldn't resist. All of the kids were laughing.

My wife threw the dish towel onto the middle of the floor. "Off sides," she said. "That'll cost you five yards."

Aaliah moved to the opposite side of the circle from Maryam looking more like a satisfied sphinx than a fallen angel. The kids' sympathies were obviously with Aaliah and not with their appointed referee.

I wondered if my pitch pipe would ever work again.

"The angel spoke to Muhammad a second time," the narrator continued.

"You had better recite," Aaliah purred.

"I do not recite," Maryam snipped back. "Can't you angels understand English?"

The pitch pipe went off again. But this time there was no flag.

"First warning for unnecessary foolishness," my wife said. "One more time and I'll throw both of you in the penalty box."

"This time machine seems to be malfunctioning," I said. "If we can't get it to fly right, we may need to abort the mission and take it in for repairs."

The narrator sighed and continued reading, "The angel embraced the Prophet tightly again and spoke to him a third time ..."

"Recite," Aaliah said.

"I am not a reciter," Maryam responded.

"The Angel embraced the Prophet again and released him, before reciting the first words of the Qur'an," Muhammad said. And then he read the actual words:

Recite in the name of your Lord who created
Created humankind from a clot
Recite and your Lord is most Generous
He taught by the pen
Taught man what he knew not. (96:1-5)

بِسْمِ اللَّهِ الرَّحْمَٰنِ الرَّحِيمِ

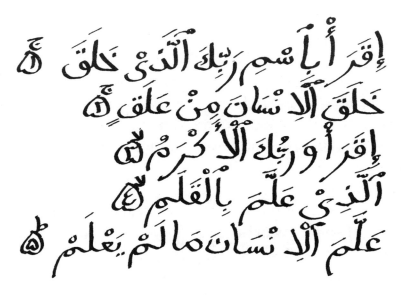

اقْرَأْ بِاسْمِ رَبِّكَ الَّذِي خَلَقَ ۝
خَلَقَ الْإِنْسَانَ مِنْ عَلَقٍ ۝
اقْرَأْ وَرَبُّكَ الْأَكْرَمُ ۝
الَّذِي عَلَّمَ بِالْقَلَمِ ۝
عَلَّمَ الْإِنْسَانَ مَا لَمْ يَعْلَمْ ۝

"The angel recited those words to Muhammad," the narrator said. "And then Muhammad repeated them, and the angel left. But Muhammad was fearful that he had lost his mind. So he got up and ran from the cave. When he left the cave he heard a voice say, 'Oh Muhammad, you are the Messenger of God, and I am Gabriel.'

"Muhammad looked to where the sound came from and saw Gabriel filling the whole horizon. And no matter in which direction Muhammad looked," read Muhammad, "he saw Gabriel filling the entire horizon."

I was glad at this point that we had decided not to do a role play. It could have really gotten out of hand.

The narrator continued reading:

"Muhammad continued down the mountain to his home. When he got there he was still shaking. He collapsed onto a couch and asked his wife Khadijah to cover him."

"Muhammad, what's the matter, Muhammad, what's the matter?"Aliyah asked.

"I'm afraid I'm going crazy," Maryam responded.

"If this keeps up, soon I may be just as crazy as some of those people you see walking around in the street claiming that God told them something."

"I don't understand, Muhammad, tell me what happened," Aliyah implored with a wide-eyed look of worry.

I expected to hear the whistle at any minute.

Maryam replied, with eyes just as wide, "I was in a cave trying to meditate, and an angel appeared and told me to read in the name of God. Then when I left the cave the angel appeared everywhere around me. He told me that he was Gabriel and that I am God's messenger. Oh Khadijah, I am afraid that I may be going crazy."

I glanced at the referee. She had stopped watching the action and was examining the markings on my pitch pipe.

"Muhammad, you are a good and responsible man," Aliyah said. "You take very good care of your family. You are so kind and honest that everyone in the community trusts you and loves you. If anyone else was saying what you are saying, like that mean old Joe Abdul down the street, they probably *would* be crazy. As a matter of fact, I've always thought that Joe was crazy, and he never even goes to the mountains. Just yesterday ...."

"Hold on," interrupted the narrator, "there's no Joe Abdul in this book."

Then I heard the pitch pipe. Not loudly this time, but at just the right tone. Maybe it would still work after all.

"First warning for unauthorized tripping," my wife said.

"Ah yes," the athlete recovered. "Let me go and speak with my cousin, Waraqah, and see what he says."

Then Ibrahim spoke Waraqah's words, "Muhammad, Khadijah has told me what happened. And I have come to congratulate you and to pray for you. God has given you a great honor. I wish that I were still a young man, so that I could be with you when your people cast you out."

"Cast me out?" Maryam looked genuinely astonished.

"That's right," Ibrahim said, while looking impressively Spock-like. "Remember what happened to Jesus. Anytime someone brings to their people what you will bring, their people cast them out."

Now it was my turn. "All right crew, you've done an excellent job. It's time to beam up to the star ship and take a break before the next episode.

"Muhammad, switch the time machine back to the present, will you? Yeah, over there. Just turn the volume knob on the amplifier. Thanks."

THE BIG DECISION

"Okay, Maryam , now you've just learned something about the fast of Ramadan that you're going to share with the rest of us."

"I have?"

"Yes, Sweetie. You've imagined yourself in the place of the Prophet Muhammad (May Allah bless him and grant him peace). Everybody in Mecca respects you and likes you. But some words from God have just come to you, and now you need to go and tell the Meccans to stop worshiping idols, and to be kind to the poor and to orphans and to women, and even to slaves. Many of the people who are now your friends are about to become very upset with you. They are going to try to hurt you and to hurt the people you love. The powerful people in Mecca are going to make life very hard for you. Eventually, even your beloved wife Khadijah (May Allah be pleased with her) will die, and the Meccans will drive you out of the city. What are you going to do?"

"Can I leave now?"

"No, Sweetie, you have to stay and preach to them until you are driven out."

"How long will that take?"

"Thirteen years."

"I guess they didn't have time machines back then."

"No sweetie, they didn't. And remember the rules of our game. You have to try to think like the Prophet Muhammad, which means that you are very honest and patient. So do you think you would be able to make believe that the whole thing was just a nutty dream?"

"No. But maybe I don't have to tell everybody."

"The Prophet Muhammad wondered the same thing at first, because he was a quiet man. But the angel Gabriel came back again. Tell us what he said, Mr. Narrator."

Muhammad read from the Qur'an:

You who are wrapped up in a cloak,
stand up and warn. Magnify your Lord,
Purify your clothing and steer clear of filth.
Do no favor seeking gain, and
for the sake of thy Lord be patient. (74:1-7)

"He was patient for 13 years?" Maryam asked.

"Thirteen years until he was driven out of Mecca," I replied. "And he spent another 10 years in preaching and teaching after that. No one in the history of the world ever changed a whole society in the way that the Prophet Muhammad did. But it took a long time, so he had to be very patient and also very strong."

"So I guess, if I'm honest, patient and strong like the Prophet Muhammad, I'll just have to hang around and do it. So that's why we fast in Ramadan? So we can learn to be like the Prophet Muhammad?"

"That's right, Sweetie. It's a very special holiday gift."

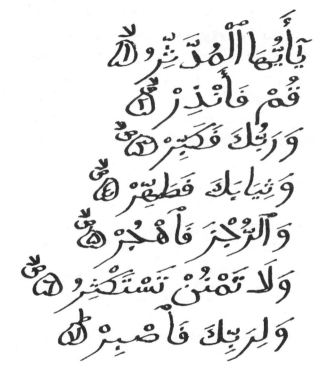

بِسْمِ اللهِ الرَّحْمٰنِ الرَّحِيمِ

يَا أَيُّهَا الْمُدَّثِّرُ ۞
قُمْ فَأَنْذِرْ ۞
وَرَبَّكَ فَكَبِّرْ ۞
وَثِيَابَكَ فَطَهِّرْ ۞
وَالرُّجْزَ فَاهْجُرْ ۞
وَلَا تَمْنُنْ تَسْتَكْثِرُ ۞
وَلِرَبِّكَ فَاصْبِرْ ۞

I recited from the Qur'an:

By the Pen and that which they write.
By the Grace of thy Lord, Thou are not
mad.
And surely thine is a reward never to be cut
off.
And you have been formed with a magnificent
character.
So you will observe, even as they observe,
which of you is being tested. **(68:1-6)**

"You know what Dad?"

"What, Sweetie?"

"I think that I'd like to try to fast during Ramadan this year."

I smiled at Maryam without saying anything. Then I glanced over at the radio to make sure that Muhammad had really turned the time machine off. Just as I thought -- he had turned the time machine knob to fast forward. Eight years old is a little early to start fasting. Muhammad started last year when he turned 12, and he probably could have waited a year or two. But little Maryam was moving entirely too

بِسْمِ اللَّهِ الرَّحْمَٰنِ الرَّحِيمِ

نٓ ۚ وَالْقَلَمِ وَمَا يَسْطُرُونَ ۝

مَآ أَنتَ بِنِعْمَةِ رَبِّكَ بِمَجْنُونٍ ۝

وَإِنَّ لَكَ لَأَجْرًا غَيْرَ مَمْنُونٍ ۝

وَإِنَّكَ لَعَلَىٰ خُلُقٍ عَظِيمٍ ۝

فَسَتُبْصِرُ وَيُبْصِرُونَ ۝

بِأَييِّكُمُ الْمَفْتُونُ ۝

fast for her old Dad. So I went over and turned off the time machine myself.

I've got nothing against growing older, understand. And I know that young people are normally in a big hurry to do it. But now that I'm in my middle years, I prefer to take it slowly, to pick up a little wisdom along the way, and maybe even to enjoy it.

THE NEW MOON

"Hey man, you're going to have to finish that nap at home." The bus driver is half smiling as he wakes me up. "The way you were grinning, you must have been having some sweet dreams."

"Good enough to charge admission," I say, rousing myself from the seat. "It's a good thing I get off at the last stop."

"I don't see as you have much choice tonight."

We both laugh.

I walk through the parking lot to my car and drive home. The house is empty. My wife and kids are visiting the folks back east. I don't check the phone messages. I just want to sleep. I make my sunset and evening prayers. Then I take my clothes off on the way to bed and dive into it. I have to step over some unidentified objects that must have fallen during the milkshake. The day after an earthquake should be good for a day off: An old-fashioned day off with no extra work. Maybe I'll take a walk in the hills with my camera. Or maybe I'll take a very long nap. I reach over to turn out the light on my bed stand and imagine the great hypnotist blowing out a candle....

"It's wonderful that you want to start fasting while you are still 8 years old, Sweetie," I said to Maryam. We were sitting in the East Bay hills and looking towards Mount Tamalpais in the west. Tamalpais is an Indian name that means "sleeping maiden." We were watching the sun set behind the sleeping maiden to see if Ramadan would start tonight.

Ramadan is one of the 12 months in the Muslim calendar, which is based on the phases of the moon. Each month begins when the new moon is born. For the beginning and end of Ramadan, Muslims still watch for the new moon in the sky in the same way that it was done 1400 years ago.

Allah says in the Qur'an:

They will ask you about the phases of the moon.
Say: "They serve as datelines for humankind and for the pilgrimage." (2:189)

This year, we went out to watch it as a family. And I had placed my camera on a tripod to take a picture of it. Maryam was very excited and looking forward to fasting this year.

بِسْمِ اللَّهِ الرَّحْمَٰنِ الرَّحِيمِ

يَسْـَٔلُونَكَ عَنِ ٱلْأَهِلَّةِ ۖ قُلْ هِيَ مَوَاقِيتُ لِلنَّاسِ وَٱلْحَجِّ ۗ

"Normally, young Muslims don't fast for the month of Ramadan until they get into their teen years," I said. "So there's no obligation for you, but go ahead and do as much as you feel comfortable with.

"The most important thing for you to learn right now, Sweetie, is about sharing the month with your family."

"That's why I want to fast," she said. "I don't want to be the only one in the house who's eating. I want to be hungry like everybody else."

"There's more to fasting than just being hungry," I said. "The idea is to learn patience, remember?"

"Oh yeah."

Everybody else was indeed patient right now. They were bundled up against the evening breeze, and searching the western sky for a special light. I thought of wise kings from the East again. Funny how that works.

"How do we learn to be patient?" Maryam asked. "Do we all sit and meditate like the Prophet Muhammad did in his cave?"

"Sort of," I answered slowly. "During the day, when I am not eating or drinking, I do feel quiet and peaceful, as if I am waiting for a word from God. Even though I work with people who are not fasting, my fast seems to keep me peaceful.

"That's a very good way to describe it, Maryam. That's probably why it's important to avoid arguments during the fast, even if people are rude toward us. Arguing back would be like leaving the cave. And even if you won the argument, you might lose something much greater."

That's when I heard the shout. They must have seen the moon. Everybody was jumping up and down, pointing and hollering. They didn't look like wise kings anymore. Now they looked like a bunch of San Francisco 49ers who had just won the Super Bowl.

Then I saw it, too. Barely visible in the fading glow of the setting sun, the new moon was shaped like a faint smile near the top of a deep-orange sky. It reminded me of a smiling cheshire cat I'd seen years ago in a cartoon movie. This smiling cat was riding the setting sun, and would soon disappear with it behind the sleeping maiden mountain. I snapped a couple of pictures of the moon from different angles, while the 49ers continued to whoop it up.

Maryam remained calm, however, looking every bit like her namesake and smiling back at the kitty-cat moon. "That's all the more reason that I should fast this year," she said. "Isn't that right, Dad? Fasting will help me to go into my own little cave and be peaceful."

"You mean like your brothers and sisters?"

"You know what I mean," she laughed. Actually, the 49ers had settled down and were walking back towards us just in time to help me carry my camera gear back down the hill.

I did know what Maryam meant, but wasn't ready to give up yet.

"You have to make sure that your cave is properly prepared first," I said. "You have to furnish it and make sure that everything is in its place."

"Why do you need furniture in a cave?" she asked.

"That's a good question, Sweetie." I didn't get the

chance to answer it.

"You've heard Daddy tell Ibrahim that his room looks like a cave, right?" Aaliah the artist chimed in.

"That's because it's a mess," Maryam said, turning up her nose. "He just throws everything all over the floor."

"Right," I said. "Do you think that an angel would come to visit you in Ibrahim's room?"

"No," Maryam answered. "But spiders might."

"Right. Or maybe rattlesnakes or grizzly bears," Muhammad laughed.

Sensing that there was no hope for him in this discussion, Ibrahim decided to take the high road. He tossed the tripod onto his shoulder and walked down the hill ahead of us.

"Is that why little Muhammad used to have nightmares sometimes, when he was sharing a room with Ibrahim?" Maryam asked.

"I don't know, Sweetie," I said. "But there could be a connection."

"All right, so how do I keep my cave from looking like Ibrahim's room?" she asked. "Can I hire a cavekeeper?"

"You probably could," Aliyah the athlete said. "But that joke sounds like one of Ibrahim's. And if you tell jokes like his, the cavekeeper might quit."

Evidently Ibrahim wasn't out of earshot because when he heard this last crack he turned and hustled back up toward us.

"Have you asked Maryam how I manage to keep such a messy room, and still make it through Ramadan without getting carried off by man-eating spiders?" he asked me.

I looked at him, and then at Maryam .

"They're afraid of the screen saver on his computer," she said.

"Huh?" now it was my turn to stare with my mouth open.

"I asked him if he was afraid of spiders crawling out from under the clothes that he throws on the floor," she explained. "He said there was nothing to

82

worry about because the screen-saver on his computer is a giant wasp that kills spiders."

I closed my mouth. Ibrahim was laughing like Mr. Spock would probably laugh if the scriptwriters would let him. Everybody else was laughing, and I chuckled a bit, too. I also made a mental note that I hadn't reminded Ibrahim to clean his room for about two days now. I used to have to yell at him to do it. Now I just tell him nicely that he will not be allowed to eat until the room is clean. That seems to work quite well, as long as I don't look in the closet.

GOOD CAVEKEEPING

"All right Sweetie," I said to Maryam . "Now that Ramadan has begun, we can start showing you how we maintain that peaceful space inside."

When we got to the front door of the house, we took off our shoes before stepping inside, hanging up our jackets, and putting the camera gear away.

"As it turns out, there are a number of things that we do in Ramadan, like housekeeping, that help us stay peaceful and patient. First, we get up before dawn to have breakfast together. Then when dawn comes and it is time to start fasting, we say our prayers together and read from the Qur'an. The morning time that we spend together helps each of us prepare a nice clean cave to meditate in all day long."

"All day long?" Maryam asked. "I don't think I'd want to stay in a cave all day long. I'd feel like a hermit."

"You've got a point there, Sweetie. I don't think

I'd like to sit in a real cave all day either, or even for part of a day. But we're not talking about a real cave. Muslims don't go off and sit in caves during Ramadan. What we try to do is keep our hearts peaceful and patient all day long, no matter what happens.

"When we say the midday prayer at just past noon, the day is already half over, and we make our hearts peaceful again for the second half of our fast. Then when we say the mid-afternoon prayer, the fast is three-quarters over, and we make our hearts peaceful again for the last quarter of our daily fast."

"But Daddy," Maryam protested, "the midday prayer comes when I am at school. There are no other Muslims there, and even if there were, we don't have a place to pray."

"I understand, Sweetie. I'm the only Muslim at my job, too. When I am at work during the day, I try to get together with Muslims who work nearby to make the midday prayer. We usually pray in someone's office, or try to find an empty conference room. When the mid-afternoon prayer arrives, I'm usually still at work, and I pray it in my office."

"What did you do when you didn't have an office? When you were working in an open cubicle?"

"I just made my prayers in the cubicle."

"Didn't people walk by and see you?"

"Yes. And it wasn't always comfortable or easy. I asked my boss, if there was a quiet place in the building where I could make my prayers. It turned out that there wasn't. So I explained that I would need to pray at my work space, and my boss understood. And that's what I did. Even though it was a little uncomfortable to just stand up and pray alone like that, I always felt better after I did it, especially during the month of Ramadan."

"I don't think I could do that at school," she said.

"I understand, Sweetie, and you may not have to. A couple of the public high schools in our city have started providing a room where the Muslim children can make the required prayers while they are at school. Maybe the people at your school will do that, too. We ought to ask.

"Anyway, after working or being at school all day, it's always nice to come back home and spend a couple of hours before the sunset meal with your family. We're all feeling nice and peaceful, and it's good to feel that together. We can go for walks, or help prepare the meal, or get ready to go out and break our fast with friends.

"The Prophet Muhammad (May Allah grant him blessings and peace) told us that Allah has reserved two rewards for people who fast. You get the first reward when you eat after fasting all day. You get the second reward when you meet Allah at the end of your time in this world.

"The first thing that happens at the end of the fasting day is that someone stands up as the western sky turns pink at sunset and chants the call to prayer. Tonight is the first night of Ramadan. So we'll let Muhammad give the call for the sunset prayer. It will help us start the month with patient and peaceful hearts."

"But Daddy," Maryam said, "We still do many of these things even when we are not fasting."

"That's true, Sweetie. But we say a lot more prayers in Ramadan, and do a lot more Qur'an read-ing. For instance, after we make the evening prayer tonight, I am going to the mosque for the special Ramadan prayers. Someone who has memorized the entire Qur'an will lead the prayer and recite one-thirtieth of the Qur'an during each night of the 30 nights in Ramadan. We also pay a lot more attention when we pray now, because we know it's a special time.

"That's the part that I want you to concentrate on during this Ramadan. Pay special attention to how it feels when we get up to eat in the morning, or when we break our fast in the evening, or when we say our prayers. Try to feel the peace, even when we go to the mosque or to other people's houses. You can fast a few days or parts of days, but don't rush.

"Take time out now to prepare a beautiful and peaceful cave in the mountain of your heart. Then, when you are 13 or 14 years old and want to go there to fast and mediate, it will be a familiar and wonderful place. And it will always be there for you. All you have to do is follow the rules of Islam, which maintain it."

I recited from Qur'an:

(Allah's Light is lit) in houses that Allah had permitted to be raised up
In which His name is mentioned.
In them He is glorified morning and evening
By people whom neither business nor trading
Distract from remembering Allah, keeping up prayer and giving charity.
They fear a day when their hearts and eyesight will be upset
Unless Allah rewards them for the finest things they have done
And gives them even more out of His bounty.
Allah provides for anyone He wishes without reckoning. (24:36-38)

بِسْمِ اللَّهِ الرَّحْمَٰنِ الرَّحِيمِ

فِي بُيُوتٍ أَذِنَ اللَّهُ أَن تُرْفَعَ وَيُذْكَرَ فِيهَا اسْمُهُ لَا يُسَبِّحُ لَهُ فِيهَا بِالْغُدُوِّ وَالْآصَالِ ۩

رِجَالٌ لَّا تُلْهِيهِمْ تِجَارَةٌ وَّلَا بَيْعٌ عَن ذِكْرِ اللَّهِ وَإِقَامِ الصَّلَوٰةِ وَإِيتَاءِ الزَّكَوٰةِ يَخَافُونَ يَوْمًا تَتَقَلَّبُ فِيهِ الْقُلُوبُ وَالْأَبْصَارُ ۩

لِيَجْزِيَهُمُ اللَّهُ أَحْسَنَ مَا عَمِلُوا وَيَزِيدَهُم مِّن فَضْلِهِ

BREAKFAST OF CHAMPIONS

The ringing sound seems to grab me at some deep spot within my head. It pulls me from the bright light in my dream to the darkness of my bedroom. I grope for the telephone and mutter into it sleepily.

"Are you all right?" My wife is on the other end. They've all been watching news reports about the earthquake on television. She says the kids are crying. The networks are talking about fires out of control, collapsed freeways and hundreds or maybe thousands of casualties. I can't check what she's saying, because I don't have a TV. But I turn on my clock radio, and all I hear is music.

"Are you sure that they're talking about San Francisco?" I ask.

"Yes," she answers. "Why don't you talk to the kids and let them know you're all right?"

After we talk, I hang up and look at the ceiling. My wife and I were married in the church that I had been christened in as a child. It was my grandmother's church. She didn't own it, but she was very active in it. I had stopped attending church regularly when I reached my twenties. I decided to start again when I got married though. People were always saying that families that prayed together stayed together.

Raising a family is hard work -- especially when you have to stop acting like a kid so that you can raise your kids. I had read about Islam and thought it might give me the discipline and patience I needed. So I decided to try it. Islam didn't make it easier to be a parent. But it helped me to understand that struggling to overcome the hard parts was actually a form of worship.

The full moon smiles through the open curtains at my bedroom window. I imagine that the great hypnotist is the man in the moon.

I sink back into the pillow and realize that I still need more patience. I close my eyes and imagine that I'm a kid who imagines that he can walk on moonbeams. The great hypnotist laughs and asks, "Why don't you try it?" I think about the "magic kingdom" and all of that stuff that I used to watch on TV and in the movies when I was a kid. Someone is leading me and a bunch of other kids on a great adventure. He starts to sing, "When you wish upon a star..." The singer sounds a lot like the great hypnotist. The scene starts to blur. I wonder if I'm falling asleep or falling awake.

It's a good thing we did get everybody to bed early last night, because now that it's Ramadan, everyone has to get up at 4:30 a.m. in order to have an early meal before the fast begins.

Allah says in the Qur'an:

Eat and drink until the white thread of dawn can be distinguished by you from the black thread
of night at daybreak (2:187)

Getting people out of bed at this time of the morning can be tough. I've learned a technique for the boys, though. I just say, "It's time to eat." Then I stand aside to keep from getting trampled.

One thing I always stress to the sleepy eyes and shuffling feet at the breakfast table is that they need to drink a lot of fluids, both before they begin the fast in the morning and when they break it in the evening. Unlike most fasts that people do for diet or hygiene reasons in the U.S., the Ramadan fast is not a juice or liquid fast. And while the pace of life may slow down during Ramadan in Middle Eastern countries,

بِسْمِ اللَّهِ الرَّحْمَٰنِ الرَّحِيمِ

وَكُلُوا وَاشْرَبُوا حَتَّىٰ يَتَبَيَّنَ لَكُمُ الْخَيْطُ الْأَبْيَضُ مِنَ الْخَيْطِ الْأَسْوَدِ مِنَ الْفَجْرِ

that doesn't happen in the U.S. The active human body can go for a long time without food, but fluids are an essential part of staying healthy and functional.

So our morning meals include a lot of water and juices and fruits. This doesn't always go over well initially with the egg-and-pancake crowd. But once they figure out how much better they feel with plenty of fluids in them, the fluids and fruits become more popular.

Actually, the morning meal in Ramadan, called Suhoor, is a special time. Normally, our different school and work schedules keep us from eating breakfast together. For instance, I like to commute to work on my bicycle. The trip is 13 miles one way. During Ramadan, though, I couldn't possibly eat or drink enough keep up my bicycle commute. So I take the bus to work and spend more time with my family -- not because I leave the house any later, but because we all get up earlier.

And it isn't bad. Today the kitchen table looked like a smorgasbord with all kinds of fruits and other colorful dishes. Everybody munched away and started to wake up and chatter.

As we chattered, however, we had to keep an eye

on the clock so that we could stop eating by dawn, which comes at about 6 a.m. during the short winter days.

This isn't always easy, because Muhammad and Aliyah the athlete are both highly sociable at the table. And when they get going, all of the kids can become so involved in socializing that they forget to eat.

Today, Aliyah and Muhammad were describing a movie in which the hero obtained super powers by putting on a mask. Aliyah popped a napkin in front of her face and started wiggling around in her chair like a snake. She was laughing at Muhammad and saying, "You missed me, you missed me."

Machine-gun Muhammad, sitting across the table from Aliyah, was the bad guy. He picked up his watermelon slice, pointed it at her and shouted, "Hold still, ya little weasel. Dadadadaadadaddada."

Aliyah kept laughing and wiggling around the imaginary bullets. She started singing, "Nananana, you still missed me."

Aaliah the artist is normally uncommunicative in the mornings. But by this time she had broken into a case of uncontrollable giggles. So much so that I feared she might fall out of her chair and into the food. Then Ibrahim got into the act.

"Anybody can dodge watermelon bullets, you silly masked person. But let's see you dodge these grapefruit bombs."

He picked up a half grapefruit in each hand and began making jet fighter noises while turning the grapefruit halves upside down and waving them over the masked heroine's head.

Undaunted, Aliyah the athlete added some up-and-down moves to the side-to-side wiggling, and snarled, "No way slowpoke," at Ibrahim.

Then Aaliah the artist stopped laughing. She held up her glass of water and made a sphinx face through it, while sliding her chair back from the table. "Under-table-water-woman will now sprinkle ice water on your toes, masked person. Let's see you get out of that."

"No!," screamed Aliyah the athlete, while adding a foot-stomping motion to the side-to-side and up-and-down.

This must be why families in the Middle East 1400 years ago just spread a tablecloth on the ground instead of using tables. Normally, I would have stopped the mayhem before this, but I wanted to see what would happen. This production was much more lively than what they did last week at dinner after watching the Mighty Muffin Pocket Rockets at a friend's house.

My wife, however, was neither amused nor curious. She was extremely concerned about getting some nutrients and fluids into these kids before they started fasting. She was equally concerned that the horseplay was on the verge of sending food, plates and drinking glasses into a mess on the floor.

The look she gave me was not to be ignored. So I cleared my throat to bring the whole thing to a halt, just as Maryam jammed a banana through Aliyah the athlete's napkin mask and tore it away from her face.

"Banana baby wins again," Maryam declared. "Now quit fooling around so we can eat."

"Thank you banana baby," I said. Maryam doesn't usually participate in the crazy stuff, so everyone was stunned into a momentary silence, which gave me the perfect opportunity.

"Let me remind you young people that the reason we woke you up this early was not so you could wake up the neighbors too, but in order for you to observe Ramadan. That means peaceful and orderly behavior. Got that?"

Everyone was silent.

"Okay, you've got 15 minutes to finish eating, and 15 minutes to clean up before the dawn prayer," I continued. Al-Islam doesn't impose these time limits. But every now and then, I have to make up some of my own. Without limits, this crew would party all the way to sunrise. "Do you have any questions?"

Silence.

"Good, get started."

Throughout the meal I kept wondering if Banana Baby was a new cartoon character, or if Maryam had made it up. But it didn't seem wise to ask, so I didn't.

MORNING WORSHIP

At precisely 20 minutes before dawn, Aliyah the athlete looked at her watch and said, "We need to finish eating in 5 minutes so that we can clean up the kitchen before the dawn prayer."

"Thank you, Aliyah," said Aaliah the artist.

"You're welcome, Aaliah," the athlete replied.

I had already finished eating, so I excused myself from the table to get ready for work. As I finished dressing, I heard Muhammad reciting the call to prayer in the living room.

As with the Qur'an, the call to prayer is recited in classical Arabic. But here's what it means in English:

Allah is greater, Allah is greater
Allah is greater, Allah is greater
I testify that there is no god but Allah.
I testify that there is no god but Allah
I testify that Muhammad is the messenger
of Allah
I testify that Muhammad is the messenger
of Allah
Come to prayer, Come to prayer
Come to success, Come to success
Prayer is better than sleep, Prayer is better
than sleep
Allah is greater, Allah is greater
There is no god but Allah.

اللهُ أَكْبَرُ اللهُ أَكْبَرُ

اللهُ أَكْبَرُ اللهُ أَكْبَرُ

أَشْهَدُ أَنْ لَّا إِلَهَ إِلَّا اللهُ

أَشْهَدُ أَنْ لَّا إِلَهَ إِلَّا اللهُ

أَشْهَدُ أَنَّ مُحَمَّدًا رَسُوْلُ اللهِ

أَشْهَدُ أَنَّ مُحَمَّدًا رَسُوْلُ اللهِ

حَيَّ عَلَى الصَّلَوةِ حَيَّ عَلَى الصَّلَوةِ

حَيَّ عَلَى الْفَلَاحِ حَيَّ عَلَى الْفَلَاحِ

الصَّلَوةُ خَيْرٌ مِنَ النَّوْمِ

الصَّلَوةُ خَيْرٌ مِنَ النَّوْمِ

اللهُ أَكْبَرُ اللهُ أَكْبَرُ

لَا إِلَهَ إِلَّا اللهُ

105

Then when everyone had washed up and we had placed the prayer rugs, Muhammad gave the call for us to actually line up for prayer:

Allah is greater, Allah is greater
I testify that there is no god but Allah
I testify that Muhammad is the messenger
of *Allah*
Come to prayer, come to success
Stand up for prayer, stand up for prayer
Allah is greater, Allah is greater
There is no god but Allah.

Then Ibrahim got up to lead the prayer. And we made two rows behind him; men in one row, women in the other. We were all facing Mecca in Arabia, where God's words first came to the Prophet Muhammad. In each row we stood so close that the sides of our feet and arms touched the person next to us.

اللهُ أَكْبَرُ اللهُ أَكْبَرُ

أَشْهَدُ أَنْ لَا إِلهَ إِلَّا اللهُ

أَشْهَدُ أَنَّ مُحَمَّدًا رَسُولُ اللهِ

حَيَّ عَلَى الصَّلوةِ حَيَّ عَلَى الْفَلَاحِ

قَدْ قَامَةِ الصَّلوةُ قَدْ قَامَةِ الصَّلوةُ

اللهُ أَكْبَرُ اللهُ أَكْبَرُ

لَا إِلهَ إِلَّا اللهُ

صلَّى ٱللهُ عَلَيْهِ وَ سَلَّمَ

Then Ibrahim, said "Allahu Akbar," which means Allah is greater, and led us in prayer by reciting the opening chapter of the Qur'an:

In the name of Allah Who gives before we ask
And Who still gives and forgives when we ask for more.
All Praise is for Allah the Lord of all the worlds
Who Gives all and still forgives
The Master of the day when all debts will be paid
Thee alone do we worship
And Thee alone do we ask for help.
Guide us on the path of those who stand upright
The path of those who are full of joy.
Not of those with wrath on them
Nor of those who've gone astray. (1:1–7)

Then he continued reciting the Qur'an from another chapter:

بِسْمِ ٱللَّهِ ٱلرَّحْمَٰنِ ٱلرَّحِيمِ ۝

ٱلْحَمْدُ لِلَّهِ رَبِّ ٱلْعَٰلَمِينَ ۝

ٱلرَّحْمَٰنِ ٱلرَّحِيمِ ۝

مَٰلِكِ يَوْمِ ٱلدِّينِ ۝

إِيَّاكَ نَعْبُدُ وَإِيَّاكَ نَسْتَعِينُ ۝

ٱهْدِنَا ٱلصِّرَٰطَ ٱلْمُسْتَقِيمَ ۝

صِرَٰطَ ٱلَّذِينَ أَنْعَمْتَ عَلَيْهِمْ

غَيْرِ ٱلْمَغْضُوبِ عَلَيْهِمْ

وَلَا ٱلضَّالِّينَ ۝

In the name of Allah Who gives before we ask

And Who still gives and forgives when we ask for more.

Say: Allah is One.
Allah is Eternal
He does not have children
and was never a child
and there is none like unto Him.(112:1-4)

Ibrahim bowed at the waist, and we all bowed behind him. Then he stood up straight and we stood up. He kneeled and touched his head to the floor, and we all did the same. We continued through the prayer, thinking of Allah, and preparing a clean and peaceful place inside for meditation.

Then since we still had a lot of time before school, everybody read one-thirtieth of the Qur'an for this day of Ramadan (except for Maryam, who can't read quite that fast yet).

I headed off a little before sunrise to catch my bus to work. The bus ride seemed very long. And all of the passengers were pedaling bicycles inside of the bus. This must be a dream....

اللهُ أَكْبَرُ اللهُ أَكْبَرُ

أَشْهَدُ أَنْ لَا إِلَهَ إِلَّا اللهُ

أَشْهَدُ أَنَّ مُحَمَّدًا رَسُولُ اللهِ

حَيَّ عَلَى الصَّلَاةِ حَيَّ عَلَى الْفَلَاحِ

قَدْ قَامَةِ الصَّلَاةُ قَدْ قَامَةِ الصَّلَاةُ

اللهُ أَكْبَرُ اللهُ أَكْبَرُ

لَا إِلَهَ إِلَّا اللهُ

HARRIS-BEY CAFE

The phone is ringing again. This time it's my mother. She's concerned about the earthquake. My mom is also concerned that I might be working too hard and not getting enough rest. She would have called to check on me earlier, but she'd been caring for my ill grandmother, who, she informs me, has just passed away. We don't talk long. I tell her that the earthquake was not as serious as the TV people are saying. She sounds relieved and tells me to go back to sleep. I hang up, lie back and close my eyes.

It seems that a lot of who I am comes from the growing up that I did in my grandmother's house. Life doesn't get much better than the pot roast dinners that she served on Sunday afternoons to family and guests from the church. Heaven has to be a place where people have no time to build empires because they're too busy enjoying pot roast dinners.

Even after I embraced Al-Islam, my grandmother

was always very respectful of my faith. On her 80th celebration at the church, I gave a talk about Islam, and about how my Islamic values came from what my mother and grandmother had taught me. I even led the congregation in prayer by reciting the opening chapter of the Qur'an.

When I was young my mother used to leave me at my grandmother's when she was at work. I used to watch the magic kingdom on the television in my grandmother's living room. Right now I am remembering a religious commercial called, "Our shrinking world." The commercial would begin with a picture of the Earth. Then the narrator would talk about new methods of rapid travel such as airplanes. (There was no Internet then.) The big question at the end was something like, "Now that we can get so far so fast, do we have any place better to go?"

I seem to hear the great hypnotist's voice. He's singing again, "Slow down, you move too fast ..."

I don't really like commuting, but if you've got to do it, there's no better way than crossing over the San Francisco Bay. The view seemed even more beautiful today because of the fast. It made me thoughtful.

Allah says in the Qur'an:

Oh humankind, worship your Lord
Who created you as well as those before you
So that you might be conscious of Allah.
He (Allah) is the One Who has made the
Earth a carpet for you.
And had the sky built above you
And sent water to pour down from the sky
And brought forth fruit by means of it
as sustenance for you. (2:21-22)

The view also reminded me of the prayers of the Prophet Ibrahim and his son, Isma'il (may Allah grant them peace), who are called Abraham and Ishmael in the Bible. And in those prayers, which are in the Qur'an, I recognized the feelings, concerns and aspirations that all parents have as they struggle to raise their offspring:

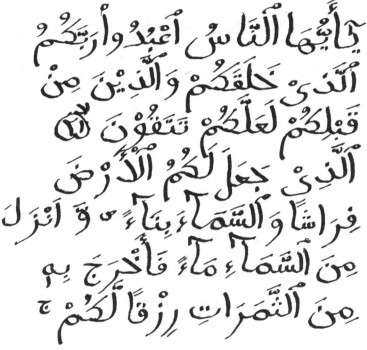

بِسْمِ اللَّهِ الرَّحْمَٰنِ الرَّحِيمِ

يَٰأَيُّهَا النَّاسُ اعْبُدُوا رَبَّكُمُ الَّذِي خَلَقَكُمْ وَالَّذِينَ مِن قَبْلِكُمْ لَعَلَّكُمْ تَتَّقُونَ ۝ الَّذِي جَعَلَ لَكُمُ الْأَرْضَ فِرَاشًا وَالسَّمَاءَ بِنَاءً ۖ وَأَنزَلَ مِنَ السَّمَاءِ مَاءً فَأَخْرَجَ بِهِ مِنَ الثَّمَرَاتِ رِزْقًا لَّكُمْ ۖ

121

And Ibrahim said: My Lord, make this countryside safe and provide any of its people who believe in God nd the last day with fruits from it.

He (Allah) said: Even anyone who disbelieves, I'll bestow benefits on for a time. Then I'll drive him on to the punishment of fire: An evil destination.

And when Ibrahim and (his son) Isma'il laid the foundations for the House (of pilgrimmage), (They prayed): Our Lord, accept this (effort) from us! Indeed You are the Alert, the Aware!

Our Lord, leave us peacefully committed to You, and make our offspring into a nation which is at peace with You. Show us our ways of worship and turn towards us.

You are so Relenting, the Merciful!

Our Lord, send a messenger in among them from among themselves who will recite Your verses to them and teach them the Book and Wisdom and will purify them.

Certainly You are the Powerful, the Wise. (2:126–129)

بِسْمِ ٱللَّهِ ٱلرَّحْمَٰنِ ٱلرَّحِيمِ

وَإِذْ قَالَ إِبْرَٰهِيمُ رَبِّ ٱجْعَلْ هَٰذَا بَلَدًا

ءَامِنًا وَٱرْزُقْ أَهْلَهُ مِنَ ٱلثَّمَرَٰتِ مَنْ

ءَامَنَ مِنْهُم بِٱللَّهِ وَٱلْيَوْمِ ٱلْءَاخِرِ قَالَ

وَمَن كَفَرَ فَأُمَتِّعُهُ قَلِيلًا ثُمَّ أَضْطَرُّهُۥ

إِلَىٰ عَذَابِ ٱلنَّارِ وَبِئْسَ ٱلْمَصِيرُ ۝

وَإِذْ يَرْفَعُ إِبْرَٰهِيمُ ٱلْقَوَاعِدَ مِنَ ٱلْبَيْتِ

وَإِسْمَٰعِيلُ رَبَّنَا تَقَبَّلْ مِنَّا إِنَّكَ أَنتَ

ٱلسَّمِيعُ ٱلْعَلِيمُ ۝ رَبَّنَا وَٱجْعَلْنَا

مُسْلِمَيْنِ لَكَ وَمِن ذُرِّيَّتِنَا أُمَّةً

مُّسْلِمَةً لَّكَ وَأَرِنَا مَنَاسِكَنَا وَتُبْ

عَلَيْنَا إِنَّكَ أَنتَ ٱلتَّوَّابُ ٱلرَّحِيمُ ۝

رَبَّنَا وَٱبْعَثْ فِيهِمْ رَسُولًا مِّنْهُمْ يَتْلُوا۟

عَلَيْهِمْ ءَايَٰتِكَ وَيُعَلِّمُهُمُ ٱلْكِتَٰبَ وَٱلْحِكْمَةَ

وَيُزَكِّيهِمْ إِنَّكَ أَنتَ ٱلْعَزِيزُ ٱلْحَكِيمُ ۝

My son Ibrahim was named after the Prophet Ibrahim (May Allah grant him peace) who prayed for the last prophet, Muhammad (May Allah bless him and grant him peace), to come in among his offspring and guide them.

Observing Ramadan gives us the opportunity not only to commemorate the guidance that came through Muhammad, but also to renew it. When we teach our children to observe it also, they can continue to renew it. Actually, that's probably true of everything you show or tell to your kids. It comes back.

For instance, I don't like to eat out much, but my kids have always loved it. They never seemed to understand my explanations about how it was too expensive. So about six years ago, I explained to them that we always go out to eat at our own family restaurant: the Harris-Bey Cafe.

Well, that came back to my wife and me one evening not long ago. When we came home, the kids would not let us in the kitchen. They said they had a surprise for us. It turned out that they had cooked dinner, and they were dressed up like waiters and waitresses. They had draped some sheets across the kitchen to separate the dining area from the cooking area, and had set up the dining area for a candlelight dinner for two. They had even made little menus, and Aaliah the artist had written "Bismillah Arrahman Arraheem" across the top in Arabic calligraphy. It means, "In the name of God, Most Gracious, Most Merciful;" or as I had taught my kids, "In the name of God Who gives before we ask, and when we ask forgives and still gives more."

The waiters and waitresses in the Harris-Bey cafe served us salad, main course and dessert. It was delicious. They put some nice music on the tape player and left the room while we ate. They sent Muhammad in from time to time to ask if we needed anything. I took a few pictures and put them in an album along with the menus.

The next day at lunch I told a friend about it. He's got kids too, and he helps run the Boy Scout troop at the mosque. He's a big and powerful man, well over 6 feet tall and 200 pounds. When he heard the story he got real quiet and looked down for a little while. Still looking down, he spoke quietly, "That's beautiful." It wasn't until I heard the emotion in his voice that I began to realize how beautiful it really was. I found myself sitting quietly also.

Then there was the time that Aaliah the artist did some Arabic calligraphy for back-to-school night at her middle school. She wanted to make a beautiful sign for the entrance to her classroom with the Muslim greeting of "Assalaamu 'alaikum" which means peace be upon you. Her teacher, who did not speak any Arabic, had no idea what it really said. I taught Aaliah the little bit of Arabic she knows, and I didn't know what it said either. Evidently, Aaliah had gotten so carried away with making beautiful letters that she hadn't concerned herself with which letters she was writing.

To this day, I have no idea what it said, but I know that it did not say "Assalaamu 'alaikum." I couldn't bring myself to criticize it, however. And since there were no complaints from the native Arabic speakers in the school, I figured it probably didn't mean anything bad. Or maybe they couldn't understand it either.

HOT BUTTON 9 MILLION

I wake up at about 3 a.m. to make a short prayer. I've been doing that for a few years now. The Prophet Muhammad (may Allah grant him blessings and peace) said that Allah descends to the heaven nearest Earth during the last third of the night and asks, "Is there anyone who calls upon Me so that I may accept him? Is there anyone who asks of Me so that I may grant him? Is there anyone who seeks forgiveness of Me so that I may forgive him?"

I really do cherish my sleep, but this seems like too good a deal to pass up. So I get up and pray. At first I used an alarm clock. Now I wake up naturally. I don't imagine a great hypnotist this time. If he knows what I know, he's probably praying, too. When I finish my prayer, I lie back down and fall asleep almost immediately.

It always seems that the first three days of fasting in Ramadan are the toughest. After that your body seems to get used to it, and you slow down your pace a little to keep things nice and even.

Also, some things begin to catch your attention, like a full moon low in the sky a little before sunrise. In addition to being beautiful, it lets you know that you are halfway through the month of fasting. Around that time I find that I am increasing my food intake during the dawn and sunset meals to keep my strength and attention up throughout the day.

Then as the moon continues to shrink in the sky, it marks your progress through the month: half moon for three-quarters through, and then smaller and smaller crescents as the end of the 30-day fast approaches. On some nights toward the end of Ramadan, I've looked at that shrinking moon and felt it was doing the same thing as my stomach. I felt as if I, the moon and all of God's creation were participating in the fast.

The last third of Ramadan is the holiest part of the month. Muslims believe it was during these final 10 days that the angel Gabriel visited the Prophet Muhammad for the first time. Some Muslims celebrate this night on the 25th and others on the 27th. Many Muslims stay up to pray and read from the Qur'an for the entire night.

We prefer to celebrate on the 27th, because that's also the day Maryam was born. Aaliah the artist was also born during the month of Ramadan. And every year when the 27th of Ramadan arrives, Maryam asks us to explain again how she and Aaliah could both have been born in the month of Ramadan, when one of them was born in May and the other in August. This year, Aliyah the athlete explained.

"It's because the Islamic calendar is based on the moon," Aliyah said. "While the calendar we normally use is based on the sun."

"Why does that make a difference?" Maryam asked.

"Because you measure the year differently," Aliyah said. "For our normal calendar, one year is the amount of time it takes for the earth to travel around the sun. It's 365 and a quarter days."

"I know that," Maryam said. "That's why we have leap years."

"But the Islamic calendar is based on the moon," Aliyah continued. "It takes about 29 or 30 days for the moon to circle around the earth, which makes up one month in the Islamic calendar. And then 12 of those months make up an Islamic year."

"How many days is that?" Maryam asked.

The lights in the room flickered, even though it was daytime and the switches were turned off. The music on the radio turned to static, and the under-sized motor on our kitchen garbage disposal gargled hungrily. It sounded like an underwater vacuum cleaner. I knew it wasn't our vacuum cleaner though, because our vacuum cleaner was unplugged and sitting in the hall closet. But it had turned itself on anyway.

As the washing machine began to fill itself with water, my first thought was "This must be an electric earthquake."

As the toaster puffed burnt crumbs and toast dust across the kitchen floor, my second thought was, "That was a stupid thought."

As all of the electric baseboard heaters in the house began to smoke, my third thought, which actually came out in words was, "Turn off the circuit breakers."

"I already did," my wife said, as sparks jumped from the door knobs to the carpet. "You really shouldn't let him use that thing in the house."

Then I looked at Ibrahim. I had been so absorbed in the discussion with Maryam that I hadn't noticed when he pulled the Hot Button 9 Million calculator out of his pocket. He says it's the only kind his school will let him use on standardized exams; something to do with the keyboard design. I've often wondered what happens at school when 30 kids pull these things out in one classroom at the same time.

Actually, the electrical disturbances didn't start until last year. Ibrahim devised a science project that used his computer to control all of the appliances in the house. The project worked so well that he not only got an "A" for it at school, but he also got extra credit for writing a program that allowed him to control the appliances remotely from his calculator. Unfortunately, the electronic hookups didn't seem to come apart as smoothly as they had gone together.

The electrical disturbances inside the house calmed down as Ibrahim deployed the collapsible static deflector that he had built for the original project. Clouds seemed to be gathering outside of the house, however, so we closed the windows and pulled down the shades to avoid stray lightning strikes.

"How many days per lunar month?" Ibrahim yelled from behind the umbrella shaped shield. He was spinning the umbrella to maximize static protection with one hand and furiously punching calculator keys with the other.

"It's either 29 or 30 days," Aliyah shouted back.

The calculator doesn't make any noise, but they had to shout anyway because the garbage disposal refused to turn off, even with the static detector deployed.

"Can you be more precise?" Ibrahim yelled again. He looked at me this time. The garbage disposal quieted down as he pointed the shield toward it. But then the vacuum cleaner, which was on his opposite side, started whirring so furiously that it sounded as if it was going to break out of the hall closet.

"I'm afraid that's it," I shrugged. Ibrahim was starting to sweat as he continued to twirl the umbrella shield while rocking it back and forth between the hall closet and the kitchen. The garbage disposal seemed to yell for attention every time he leaned toward the vacuum cleaner, and the vacuum cleaner yelled when he leaned toward the garbage disposal.

"It wants more precision," he muttered, looking at the HB 9 Million now, but still punching keys furiously.

Then an unfamiliar voice shouted, "AW SASSA-FRAS," and all of the noises stopped. The static shield stopped twirling and hung limply in Ibrahim's hand.

"Was that you?" I asked.

"Huh?" he said tiredly.

"Did you say sassafras?"

"No," he answered. "That was the HB 9 Million. It always says that when it can't solve a problem. Then it just shuts itself off."

"Oh." I really didn't know what else to say.

Ibrahim folded the static shield back into its pocket-sized container. The rest of us opened shades and windows, except for my wife, who turned the electricity back on.

"How many days in an Islamic year?" Maryam asked again.

"It's a little bit more than 350 days long," I answered quickly. "The Islamic year is almost two weeks shorter than the solar year. That's why the Islamic holidays come at different times of the year on our calendar. They come about 10 days earlier each year."

"That means in four years, four of us will have birthdays all in the same month," Muhammad said.

"What do you mean?" Maryam asked.

"Ibrahim and Muhammad were both born in December," Aliyah answered.

"Wow," Maryam said. "How often do the four of us have birthdays in the same month?"

"About every 30 years," I blurted as Ibrahim

reached for his pocket. "I figured it out once but I don't remember exactly.

"We won't be able to figure it exactly until we get a precise figure for the number of days in a month," I added, while looking directly at Ibrahim.

He looked back at me. Nodded. And let the dread machine slip back into his pocket.

ON THE EVE OF THE 'ID

The family plan for celebrating the 27th day of Ramadan this year was to go to a fast-breaking dinner at the mosque. These are wonderful events that occur throughout the fasting month. Normally, everyone brings food and enjoys a big potluck dinner. Often during the month, families visit each other's homes to break the fast together. In some ways, every evening in Ramadan becomes a celebration. You have to be careful though: One year I went to a few too many of these celebrations and found that I was actuallly gaining weight. My clothes were getting uncomfortably tight and I had to put myself on a diet for the rest of the month.

This year, however, we hadn't been able to get around as much as in previous ones, so we were really looking forward to a nice get-together at the mosque this evening. As the day drew to an end, the boys were especially excited about it, because they had been cutting grass and shrubs outside the mosque since noon, as part of a Boy Scout service project.

After the service project, as I drove the boys home to clean up for the evening, I realized that Ramadan was almost over. I wanted to get in a few more time machine trips before it ended. So I broached the subject after the mid-afternoon prayer. But there were no takers, not even for a home-grown Star Trek episode. Everybody was more into napping and doing quiet things. I didn't push it because, I actually felt the same way myself. Role playing is for fat bellies, not fasting ones.

Even after we went to the mosque, ate, hung out with our friends and made our prayers, nobody really wanted to stay up late. They knew that wake up time would be at 4:30 in the morning.

Starting after the 27th night, people go out after sunset to try to spot the new moon again, which signals the end of Ramadan and the beginning of the following month, Shawwal. Then we can start sleeping "late" again. We still get up at dawn to say our morning prayers, but we don't have to get up an hour before dawn in order to eat.

This year, the last days of Ramadan fell during the school and work week, so we didn't have time to go out and sight the moon. We just called the mosque at night and listened to a telephone recording that lets us know whether or not the moon has been sighted. Even when the weather is cloudy and the moon is not sighted, the fast ends officially 30 days after it starts. The first day of Shawwal is a big community feast day, which is called 'id al-fitr in Arabic.

As usual, my wife spent the last nights of Ramadan making colorful matching outfits for herself and the girls, as well as stunning African print shirts for the boys and me. I don't know where she got the energy. She didn't listen to me when I said that the outfits we wore last year would do fine.

She usually runs around buying gifts for everyone to exchange on the feast day, as well. This year, however, we had a very busy month, and I talked her into simply getting nice cards with Islamic calligraphy on them for everyone. I suggested that we put the money we would have spent on gifts into the cards and let the kids buy their own gifts. Ramadan can get expensive if you have a big family.

Every now and then the dread thought occurs to me that someday the Ramadan celebration in the U.S. might become as heavily commercialized as the Christmas season. But then I tell myself that the 30 days of fasting should help to prevent that.

I HATE WALKMANS

I wake up again and robins are singing. It's time for the dawn prayer. I get up and wash and then take my prayer rug into the back yard to make the prayer. When my prayer is over, I take a seat in the old garden chair that lives in my back yard and faces the eastern hills. There's a glow over the eastern hills but it's still dark.

I close my eyes, but don't fall asleep. I'm trying to imagine the great hypnotist. I want to ask him about my grandmother. But he doesn't show up this time. I close my eyes even tighter. Oh well, the good thing about hanging out in your back yard before sunrise is that you can do whatever silly thing you feel like doing and nobody can see you. I feel like taking a deep breath and imitating a balloon. So I do. I am just getting all nice and balloony when who should pop into my imagination but the great hypnotist. "Look here, I don't have time to talk with you now," he says. The new arrival is serving up a heavenly pot roast dinner. Just the aroma has everybody lining up, and I certainly don't want to miss mine. It smells so good that you could probably smell it too, if you'd cut out that dumb balloon imitation."

Easy for him to say. Then I do start to smell it. And it does smell familiar. I lay back in my chair and relax. It smells and feels like a Sunday afternoon and I'm laughing with friends on the steps of my grandmother's brownstone house on Union Street ....

On the morning of the feast day, we got up, said our prayers and ate breakfast during the daytime for the first time in 30 days. We then got all dressed up and headed for the convention center, where the 'id prayers and festival were held. On feast days, people from all the different community mosques get together, and the crowd is much too big for any one mosque.

We arrived at nine in the morning to make the 'id prayer. Before the prayer, each family donates enough money to feed one poor person for each family member. The donation is also thought of as an atonement for our mistakes during the fasting month. Fourteen hundred years ago, people actually donated food, and in some places they probably still do. But today in the U.S. we give money instead.

We made our prayers, and then sat on our prayer rugs to hear the sermon. When the sermon was over, the festival really started with rides, games, food and vendors, just like an amusement park. Figuring the kids will want some money to spend, my wife and I pulled them aside and gave them their cards and money.

We told them that these were their 'id gifts, which wasn't exactly true. My wife agreed with me that we could give the kids cards with money this year, but she also insisted on surprise gifts, which were waiting at home. Funny how that works.

While handing out the cards, I asked the kids what they had learned this year from the Ramadan fast.

"You always tell us that we shouldn't waste food because other people are starving," Muhammad said. "Well now we know what it feels like to be hungry and thirsty. And we know how good it feels to be able to eat and drink."

Everyone seemed to agree, including Maryam who had only fasted for a few days.

"It is really terrible," she said, "that there are so many people in the world who are fasting all the time because they don't have any food to break their fast with."

I just nodded my head. There didn't seem to be a whole lot to add. I gave everybody a hug, and then decided to go for a walk. I'm not much for crowds. I like seeing people for a while, then I like to go somewhere quiet and gaze off into the distance.

As I started on my way, the sounds of people walking, talking and laughing faded into the distance. It seemed that some of the footsteps were still with me, however. The persistent sound was a little to my right. I looked in that direction and saw Maryam smiling up at me.

"Nice day, isn't it?" she said, taking hold of my hand. "Can I walk with you?"

"Sure Sweetie," I smiled.

"How old were you when you started fasting, Daddy?"

"32."

"32? Why did you wait so long?"

"I was brought up in a Christian church."

"So why did you become Muslim?"

"When I was little, your grandmother used to tell me that there was only one God, and that all of the different religions in the world belonged to that one

143

God. One day I read that same thing in a very old book, which was the Muslim Qur'an. And that Qur'an still had all of the prophets and events that I had grown up with from the Bible. So I decided to follow it."

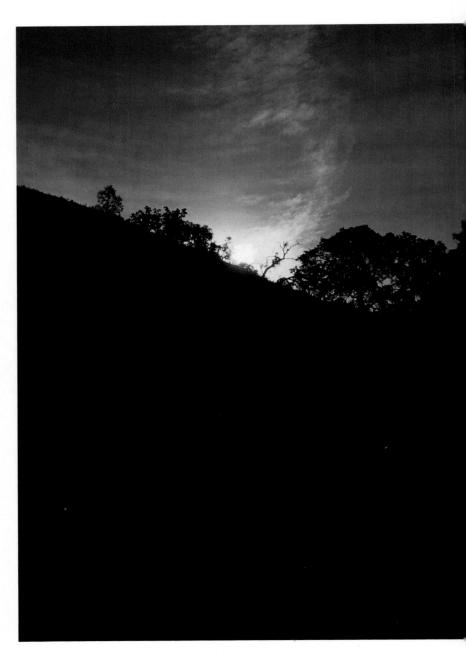

I recited from the Qur'an:

In the name of Allah Most Gracious, Most Merciful
Those who believe and those who are Jews, Christians and Sabeans,
Anyone who believes in Allah and the Last Day and acts honorably
No fear will lie upon them nor need they feel saddened. **(2:62)**

"I also liked it because of the five daily prayers, the fasting and the other disciplines that we follow. The daily discipline and activity seemed to make my religion just as important as other things I do every day, like working, sleeping and eating. I liked that."

"But you have a Muslim name," she said. "Did you change your name after you became Muslim?"

"No, Sweetie. My father's father joined an African-American religion about 60 years ago called Moorish Science. It included ideas from both Christianity and Islam. The Moorish Science Temple of America was founded in 1913 by Noble Drew Ali, an African-American who had traveled in Africa.

بِسْمِ اللَّهِ الرَّحْمَٰنِ الرَّحِيمِ

إِنَّ الَّذِينَ ءَامَنُوا وَالَّذِينَ هَادُوا وَالنَّصَارَىٰ وَالصَّابِئِينَ مَنْ ءَامَنَ بِاللَّهِ وَالْيَوْمِ الْءَاخِرِ وَعَمِلَ صَالِحًا فَلَهُمْ أَجْرُهُمْ عِندَ رَبِّهِمْ وَلَا خَوْفٌ عَلَيْهِمْ وَلَا هُمْ يَحْزَنُونَ ۝

"Back then, African-Americans often were not allowed in white churches or white schools. They couldn't get most jobs, and many of their parents and grandparents had been slaves. The names they had been given were the names of their slave masters. And their religion had been taught to them by their slave masters, also. They wanted to get away from slavery, and poverty and racism. One of the things many of them did was to join other religions, like Moorish Science.

"That's where our last name, Harris-Bey, came from. Harris was the slave master's name. Many Moorish Americans added the Muslim name Bey after their slave names. So your great-grandfather changed his family name from Harris to Harris-Bey, when he joined the Moorish Science Temple.

"Moorish Science is named after the Moors. The Moors were African Muslims who helped to bring Europe out of the Dark Ages. And as it turns out, many of the slaves who were brought to America were Muslims from Africa."

"Did the Moorish Americans fast during Ramadan?"

"I don't think so. It was probably difficult for

African-Americans to find the Arabic Qur'an back then, or even English translations of it. I learned about the Qur'an when I was studying at a university. I was only the second person from either my mother's family or my father's family who had the opportunity to graduate from college."

"So what about the Muslims from other countries? Do they already know all about Islam?"

"No Sweetie. We're all discovering Islam. The Muslims from other countries know all about how to practice Islam in a country where just about everyone else is Muslim. They don't have to think about it much because everyone around them is doing it. But many of them have trouble when they come to a place like the U.S., where so many different people live together. The Muslims who were born here, on the other hand, may be new to Islam, but we already know how to work and live with many different kinds of people. So we're all discovering how to be Muslims in America.

"In some ways, that's what the Prophet Muhammad did (May Allah grant him blessings and peace). He didn't start to learn Islam until he was 40 years old. And then for 13 years he practiced in a society where most of the people were not Muslim."

"What does the word Muslim mean?" Maryam asked.

"It means someone who submits to God's will."

"Doesn't everybody have to do that, including Christians?"

"That's what the Qur'an says Sweetie:"

Virtue does not mean for you to turn your faces towards the East and West
But virtue means one should believe in God, the Last Day, angels, the Book and prophets;
And no matter how he loves it, to give his wealth away to near relatives, orphans, the needy, the wayfarer and beggars and for freeing slaves;
And to keep up prayer and pay the welfare-tax;
And those who keep their word whenever they promise anything;
And are patient under suffering and hardship and in time of violence.
Those are the ones who are trustworthy, and they are the God-conscious. (2:177)

بِسْمِ اللَّهِ الرَّحْمَٰنِ الرَّحِيمِ

لَّيْسَ الْبِرَّ أَن تُوَلُّوا۟ وُجُوهَكُمْ قِبَلَ الْمَشْرِقِ وَالْمَغْرِبِ وَلَٰكِنَّ الْبِرَّ مَنْ ءَامَنَ بِاللَّهِ وَالْيَوْمِ الْءَاخِرِ وَالْمَلَٰٓئِكَةِ وَالْكِتَٰبِ وَالنَّبِيِّۦنَ ۖ وَءَاتَى الْمَالَ عَلَىٰ حُبِّهِۦ ذَوِى الْقُرْبَىٰ وَالْيَتَٰمَىٰ وَالْمَسَٰكِينَ وَابْنَ السَّبِيلِ وَالسَّآئِلِينَ وَفِى الرِّقَابِ وَأَقَامَ الصَّلَوٰةَ وَءَاتَى الزَّكَوٰةَ ۖ وَالْمُوفُونَ بِعَهْدِهِمْ إِذَا عَٰهَدُوا۟ ۖ وَالصَّٰبِرِينَ فِى الْبَأْسَآءِ وَالضَّرَّآءِ وَحِينَ الْبَأْسِ ۗ أُو۟لَٰٓئِكَ الَّذِينَ صَدَقُوا۟ ۖ وَأُو۟لَٰٓئِكَ هُمُ الْمُتَّقُونَ ﴿١٧٧﴾

I felt as though I'd been doing a lot of preaching and decided to just be quiet for a while and appreciate the sunshine. I personally don't like being evangelized and preached to. So when I catch myself doing it, I try to knock it off. But I'm not always successful. Poor Maryam had just asked a couple of questions, and probably felt as if her little mind had been pummeled into submission.

"Why do we do everything in Arabic?" Maryam interrupted my thoughts. She sure had a lot of questions. I started to wonder who was pummeling whom.

"Why don't we just pray and read the Qur'an in English?" Maryam continued. "Then we wouldn't have to learn Arabic."

"You're right, Sweetie," I answered. "We could learn about all of the things we need to do in our religion by reading about them in English. Then we could do those things and we would probably be very good people. Since Arabic is not our first language, we already do most of our studying in English. And most of the Muslims in the world are like us, because they did not grow up speaking Arabic. But there is another part of the religion that is very important, and you can't learn it from translations."

"What's that?" Maryam asked.

"It's something that the Christians call communion. It's a religious ceremony where each person remembers that God is not just outside of them, but also inside of them. Many Christians do this in a church ceremony where they eat a small piece of bread and maybe take a sip of wine. It can be very simple. The idea is what's important. I remember doing it in your great-grandmother's church with soda crackers and grape juice.

"For the Christians who take communion, the bread and wine remind them of the body and blood of Jesus (Peace be upon him). So when they perform this ceremony, they are taking God's word into themselves, and reminding themselves that's who they are already. It's a special ceremony, which they do in church. In some churches people purify themselves beforehand by confessing their sins to a priest.

"In Islam we make our communion whenever we recite the Qur'an in Arabic. When we recite from the Qur'an as it was originally revealed to Prophet Muhammad (May Allah grant him blessings and peace), we are reciting God's words just as our prophet heard them and then repeated them. It's a special ceremony, and we do it very often. Five times a day for the required prayers, and even more often if we do extra prayers or if we just recite the Qur'an. We purify ourselves beforehand by washing with water.

"Our communion continues to grow stronger as we learn more of the Qur'an and learn to understand it better. It's like taking some time out of your day and spending it with God. A person who learns to recite the entire Qur'an by heart is called a Hafiz, which also means a guardian. That person becomes a guardian of God's word.

"We use a book with words written in it to help us learn and remember God's words. But Muhammad didn't use a book with written words. He used his heart, and he was the first Hafiz of the Qur'an. If we really want to be close to Allah like Muhammad was, we need to do the same thing.

"The Prophet Muhammad said that the excellent Muslim is someone who prays as if he can see God. And even if he can't really see God, the excellent Muslim knows that God sees him.

"There's a social side to this, too," I continued. "Muslims all over the world speak Arabic, and ..."

"God bless you," a homeless woman smiled at us. She had children with her and was carrying a cardboard sign, which said they had no food. I was so absorbed in my own preaching that we had almost passed without noticing her.

"God bless you," she repeated, still smiling.

I reached in my pocket and gave her some change. Maryam looked at me and fidgeted with the dials on her walkman. She pulled the earphones out of her pocket and put them on.

I never have liked walkmen. I mentioned that to Aaliah the artist the other day, and she responded that the proper word is walkmans. "Walkmen are men who walk," she said.

I still don't like them. They look like mind-control machines to me. But then again, I'm the kind of guy who refuses to watch television. I slam-dunked our last TV into the trash can. When TV programs start showing positive images of African Americans on a regular basis, especially of African-American men, I might reconsider. In the meantime, I'll keep making my own images, which is how I got into storytelling.

As for walkmen ... excuse me, walkmans ... the

only reason that I let my kids use them is because of a grudging compromise with their mom. She says I overdo it at times. I really have no idea what she means. But a guy has to make some concessions every now and then to keep the peace.

I stopped musing, as Maryam took the earphones off, stepped toward the homeless lady, gave her the entire $10 'id gift, and said, "God bless you, too."

The woman was both moved and surprised by Maryam's generosity. So was I. It may be once a year that Maryam gets her hot little hands on that much money all at once. And when she gets it, she spends it very carefully.

Nora Maryam took my hand and smiled at me as we continued our walk.

"That's what the Prophet Muhammad would have done (May Allah grant him blessings and peace)," she beamed.

"How do you know?" I asked.

She touched her walkman triumphantly and said, "I took a ride in my time machine and asked him."

"Wait just a minute," I protested. "The Qur'an doesn't say to give all of your money to the poor. You still need to keep enough to take care of your own needs."

"Of course." she smiled. "But I don't need that money to take care of my needs."

"No?" I asked, mouth hanging open.

"Uh-uh," she replied, still smiling and leaning against my arm. "That's what daddies are for."

A TASTE FOR POT ROAST

I awake as a sparkling sunrise steals over the eastern mountains and coaxes my eyelids open. I sit and enjoy the sunrise for a while. Then it occurs to me to turn on the radio and make sure that today is a day off. I had a bunch of crazy dreams last night. Maybe I ought to write them down.

I turn the radio on to hear John Coltrane's rendition of "My Favorite Things." I listen for a while and then turn the tuning knob in search of a news station. Stevie Wonder's voice interrupts my search. He's singing about treating himself to the "pretty places" in his head. I laugh out loud this time. It's obviously a day off. I wonder if Mr. Wonder and the great hypnotist have similar job descriptions. I decide that they probably do, and that I've got to get one of those gigs myself. The first thing that I'm

162

going to do is write down all of these dreams I had last night. When my kids get home, maybe I'll tell them a story about my dreams. If Allah so wills it, my dreams might even come true. I have to write quickly, though, before I get too hungry to concentrate. Man, am I in the mood for pot roast.

The End

Now that I've written this book, I must admit to a certain peace of mind and would recommend the exercise to other parents. Think of it. If you do something like this, your kids will still be able to pick up a book and read what you were always telling them, even when you're no longer around to keep saying it.

PHOTOGRAPH LEGENDS

Front cover: Crescent moon at sunset over Coyote Hills in Fremont, CA.

Page 2: BART (Bay Area Rapid Transit) train entering Rockridge Station in Oakland, CA.

Page 29: Halftone of cover photo.

Page 37: Oakland Bay Bridge, seen from Tilden Park in Berkeley, CA.

Page 38: San Pablo Bay, seen from Tilden Park.

Page 40: Sunset on highway 880 in Fremont.

Page 73: Sunset over San Francisco, seen from El Cerrito, CA.

Page 74: Sunset over Mount Tamalpais, seen from El Cerrito.

Page 75: Birth of new moon for the month of Ramadan in 1995, seen from El Cerrito.

Page 109: Moonrise in Tilden Park.

Page 110: San Francisco skyline, seen from Tilden Park.

Page 112: Moonrise in Fremont.

Page 145: Dawn at Pinnacles National Monument in California.

Page 146: Approaching sunrise at Pinnacles.
Page 148: Sunrise at Pinnacles.
Back cover: Oakland Bay Bridge, seen from Tilden Park.

REFERENCES

Several translations were consulted for English meanings of Quranic passages. The ones used most often were:

1. The Noble Qur'an, T.B. Irving, 1992, Amana Books.

2. The Holy Qur'an, 'Abdullah Yusuf 'Ali, 1989, Amana Corp.

3. The Message of the Qur'an, Muhammad Asad, 1984, Dar al-Andalus.

4. The Holy Qur'an, Maulana Muhammad Ali, 1973, Specialty Promotions.

Primary sources for biography and sayings of the Prophet Muhammad (may Allah grant him blessings and peace) as they appear in this book include:

1. MUHAMMAD his life based on the earliest sources, Martin Lings, 1983, Inner Traditions International.

2. A Manual of Hadith, Maulana Muhammad Ali, (no date given), Ahmadiyya Anjuman Ishaat Islam.

Calligraphic design for the names Allah and Muhammad came from:

1. Islam for beginners, N.I. Matar, 1992, Writers and Readers Publishing.

صَلَّى ٱللهُ عَلَيهِ وَ سَلَّمَ